Lodestar
New and Selected Poems

Nagueyalti Warren

Dedicated to all the stars and black lights—

Those ultraviolet, infrared, radiant beings

Whose fluorescent essence reflects the black

Experience yesterday and today—

Shine on!

Table of Contents

Present Tense

Past Tense

Lodestar

in a galaxy of stars

spangling across a midnight sky

you are my guiding light

polar axis—mc squared

my one to the first power

you brought me from the bowels

of muddy deep river country

south of hell

you pointed up the freedom train's

conductor stealing through dark trees

along starlit streams

you just kept on shining

high up there— Holy

shine on me

shine in me

ancient sagacious eye of God

shine in me

Dear Harriet,

Araminta Ross little brown baby,

Enslaved almost two-hundred years ago.

Who knew you'd be warrior, you maybe?

You realized people thought you were slow.

Slaver hit and miss, your head gets the iron

Causing hypersomnia, you must suffer.

Spirit would show you the way to Zion.

Slavery made you braver and tougher.

You became yourself when you named yourself.

You needed freedom, left your man running.

You came back Moses, to get what you left.

You feared not for your head they were gunning.

Thank you, black woman Union Army spy,

Railroad conductor unafraid to die!

Dear Frederick,

Augustus Washington Bailey enslaved

Chattel on Maryland's Eastern Shore in

Circa 1817, born brown skin

Snatched from mother's arms making her grief crazed.

You grew strong, went along, learned to behave

Learned to read and to write, ran away, then

Caught and beaten you fought back poised to win.

Your fist for freedom was slavery's stave.

You followed the North Star and published it.

Spoke of striking the first blow for freedom.

Asked what to the slave is the 4th of July.

In Haiti you saw Africa's Spirit.

Ambassador: liberty and wisdom.

Your Afro style took black folk years to try.

Dear Isabella,

Baumfree Isabella you would be free

To make your journey and tell your own truth.

Baby Sophia in arms, you will see

Liberty. Walk away from stolen youth.

Your children snatched from your maternal hands

You used the law, sued a white man, and won.

Your son's brainwashed rejection hurt your plans.

Peter's foolishness aside, he's your son.

Once you saw light, knew what yours was to do.

Walk the talk, spread words, speak truth to power.

Many heard you, your reputation grew

Giving women power taking the hour.

Standing tall before all claiming freedom

Sojourner Truth's Spirit inspired wisdom.

Frederick Douglass to Three Young Men, Waiting

Do not stand beneath the live oak tonight.

Men like you should rage, rage against the wrong.

Rage, rage against the rope-burned limbs and fight!

As wise young men you must not yield to fright.

With powerful fists make a freedom gong.

Do not stand beneath the live oak tonight.

Men arm yourselves against the hooded knights

The outcome you desire won't take too long.

Be encouraged, run from darkness to light.

You inhabit land about to ignite

in murder, mayhem, to kill freedom's song.

Do not stand beneath the live oak tonight.

A whip-poor-will sings its warning: midnight.

Find the cacodemon, join the throng.

Rage, rage against the rope-burned limbs and fight!

Sinister place of bloody roots invites

a response: bear arms and battle the strong.

Do not stand beneath the live oak tonight

Rage, rage against the rope-burned limbs and fight.

Mississippi Woods

If woods could talk

Wonder what would they say?

Would they give away dark secrets:

Tell of night murders by knights in white sheets

Or hounds chasing fleeing, freedom-bound men?

If woods could talk

Would they tell of burning flesh?

Would they say how black blood

Fertilized their roots?

Woods won't talk

But ancient tree trunks

Hold secrets of the South

In these Mississippi woods.

Parchment

Cotton

fields

at

Parchman

Penitentiary

form

neatest,

longest

rows

of

plants

on

God's

green

earth.

Black

men

required

to

walk

the

line

bending

always

to

a

white

cotton

boll.

New

inmates

careful

not

to

prick

their

fingers

move

slowly.

Old

prisoners'

calloused

hands

not

caring

about

thorns

move

rapidly.

Deviations

left

or

right

not

allowed

straight

ahead

they

must

keep

moving

close

to

ground

heads

bent

backs

round.

A

parchment

diploma

awaits

those

who

come

to

end

of

time.

Summer Nights

After sunset in summers of my youth

Grown folks would sit outside talking laughing,

Telling tall tales lies making up the truth

What they knew of John stepping out passing

Or Sue helping Jean and her baby blue

When Jean didn't know what or how to do.

We play in smokey moon shadows, capture

Fireflies in mayonnaise jars, *Last tag,*

Last tag, you're it! We hide out in rapture

Ollie, ollie, oxen free running legs

Meet by sweet gum tree our feet in clover

Honeysuckle night blooming jasmine air

We sleep on creaking porch swings with Rover

In muggy nighttime heat without a care.

Snapshots

Strawberry summer sun beaming down
Around grandma's ole straw hat
Her hands pushing bushes back
Bees buzzing flies asking to die
Flying around grandma's ole straw hat.
She put her bucket down half full

Strawberry juice oozes sweet smells
In that southern summer strawberry sun.
Law chile it's hot too day!
Grandma'd say wiping her face
On her starched white apron.
She'd grab her bucket, snatch away my berry-stained hands.

Quit eatin'now! You gonna have the runs.
Girl start puttin' them berries
In this here bucket.
Sun shining—bees droning
Flies getting on my five-year-old nerves

Grandma would smile, wipe sweat off my nose
Soon we'd be home.

Evening breezes crossing our front porch
Announce grandma's fried chicken
To the whole of Gamble Valley
You could smell the pepper!

When dinner's done, we really have fun
Sharing our favorite thing:
Bowls of glorious golden strawberry cobbler
From a great black-iron pan bubbling bright red juices.

Killing Winter

Hog killing time was almost as horrendous

As the midnight Sheriff Butts drug Big Black River

Fishing out a huge green/gray whale, I thought.

Then I saw human eyes popped, body parts missing.

The stench rising from the bloated body smelled like hog guts.

They dragged it by shoeless feet mumbling, *nigger*!

I wondered how they could tell.

Nobody cut it to let blood out like grandpa did the hog.

Swimming

Soft southern girls with long brown legs

Narrow feet and slim behinds

Fat black plaits or skinny rows of braids

Never swam in smoldering summers of youth.

Couldn't swim.

How could a little lady undress herself

Slip naked into a muddy swimming hole

Like her brothers did—with wild abandoned glee

Exposing their private parts, comparing sizes

Yet keeping a sharp eye on trees watching

For any landowner who might appear

Scanning bushes for a shotgun barrel

Aimed in their direction.

Till's Death Did Us Part

Grand grandmothers and Great grandfathers

Go with grandiose memories of childhood

Summers spent in the deep South where they

Let us run wild and free in the woods, away

From store front churches liquor store corners

Street cars street gangs & other such kifo

That steal a child's breath.

Where they loved us, rocked us, prayed over us

Overfed us, kept us from an unknown, unseen

Unspoken of harm— keeping us from going

To town because we didn't say yes sir or yes ma'am.

Keeping us each summer until 1955 when fear paralyzed

Causing trips down South to cease.

Our great grands journeyed North looking strange

Under tall buildings, loving us still but being so

Out of place and us with no space to run.

School Daze

Morning appeared suddenly slapping

Sun rays around the pink lace twin-bed room

Seeming to shout: Get up, get out of bed!

Today is the day National Guards will lead the way

Inside the school where blacks and whites

Will break the Golden Rule.

Today you will be hated & you will hate back

But walk tall, make history despite rocks

Inside your stomach & ice cubes in your throat

That will not melt.

Blackberry Wine

Dark, it was black where fat Walley stood
Starkly against artificial night inside the barn.
Martha moved backward, tripped over hay
Jim, Tom, Herman, Bill White's boys
Held her down, kept her motionless.

Down fat Walley came, came his alabaster fingers
Clutching her blackberry breast, came, pork-smelling
Breath heaved in her flaring nostrils, came shooting
His white lightning into unlit corners of her/self.
Someone called the boys. Bill White's boys let go.

Ran but fat Walley was coming. Martha didn't weep
She didn't moan. Her arms came up above her head
Fingered a pitchfork and brought it down through
Fat Walley's red neck. Fat Walley rolled away.
Martha gazed upon the Red Sea seeping into hay

Opened the barn door, walked with blackberry juice
Staining her dress into Indian summer sun.

A Nature Poem

Miss Sunrise comes cracking her whip through

Tall pines. A fowl choir serenades the

New day. Sun, burning suddenly scarlet

Moves people quickly across red clay fields.

In this Miss Morning, this, a nature poem

Not about trees, birds, or early sunshining,

Is a poem about the nature of an

Early sunrising bringing ebony

Hands to ivory rows of cotton bolls

Burning heat, sweat, and maybe death

Before sunset— this nature is a killing one

With birds singing, pines growing tall.

New day mornings cannot change nature

Ole Miss's cracking whip or cottonflowers blooming.

Deep River

Pulsating brown like people

You shipped down

Down your riverbanks.

Deep river, languid, deceptive:

Friend to Huck and Jim

Enemy to families washed apart.

Deep river, who wants to cross over

When it's all the same?

Only thing changing is the name.

Tenn a see klan on both sides

And North and South

Of your gaping river mouth.

Deep, muddy/bloody, silent, guilty river.

Deep river, sinful river.

Where does one cross over

Into Canaan Land?

Silver Rights

The girls and the boys stood side by side
white spittle staining their round brown
freshly open faces and starched smiles.

Looking over picket mothers in a line
Soprano voiced these soldiers sang
We, O, we shall not be moved just like

Just like Lana blood oozing from a head wound
Would not be moved when called *nigger*
Would not from the lunch counter move

To eat at the Colored hole in the wall out back
Just like a tree planted by the rivers of water
That stubborn bleeding skinny girl would not.

Just like Willie Peacock would not stop
Going into town, praying on courthouse grounds
Police dogs at his back ready to attack the boy
On bended knees insisting he was free.

Glory Hallelujah.

The boys and the girls who would not stop

Went marching straight as trees

Into the valley and shadow of death.

Coretta

Summer finds her pregnant again
heat rash zizgags her long neck.

She sings a lullaby to Yoki who gurgles
fat fingers find her baby teeth.

Martin for dinner again is late.
Cabbage and pork chops wait.

Her lemon pie runs, and yellow kitchen
steams like southern sun, a spotless spot.

Walter Cronkite drones on back
and white when

Thunder not from clouds but crowds
of white not rain but insane hate

and fear erupts. Through smoke she sees
her willow blue vase—grand heirloom—

shattered in the rubble of the picture
window blown to tiny fragments.

She watches him rush to her side.
she whispers, *dinner is ruined.*

     II
Black people come with guns and bats
Men prepared to strike back.

His hand halts them, says
don't go so low. Let us pray.

They pray through clenched teeth.
Armed black men don't go away

They board up plate glass window hole.
Firearms ready these men will stay.

     III
In their room he rocks her to sleep.
She dreams of pink sand beaches

where gulls glide on turquoise sea.

In her dream she promises him

from danger she will never turn back or flee.

Lorraine

Laughter.

On the balcony
Mirth erupts
From his settled soul.

Satisfied, loved, loving
Brothers break bread
Crack jokes.

Spring's pea-green sprouts
Erupt, dogwoods bloom.

Tiny clouds like balloons
Pop at dusk, pop, pop.

He falls.

Laughter choked.
In his throat rising blood.

The Allens

Light bright and nice enough

To everyone in the 50s.

Worked in white folk's homes

Knowing things would change.

Sam Cooke stirring souls

Saying it was so.

Their time—light skin, good hair

Closer to white than to black—

Soon it would be heyday for their hue.

Imagine their incredulity when

Suddenly light skin was verboten,

When black skin was suddenly in.

Black power to the black-skin folk.

Dark as wine super fine

Sent whites looking for exotics

Blackberry skin napped up hair.

After all this time to not be black enough.

How crazy are white folk the Allens mused,

Then shrugged, wondering how insane are we?

Strut

When we move to Pico, I attend South Ranchito School,

the only black among the pink and brown kids in class.

Theresa Gonzales warns about kids but not about our teacher,

tall, thin, green-eyed mean, whose only joy is to make us work.

Hal calls me a *Negro slave* in social studies, making me cry

before my uppercut to his pug nose, draws blood. Grandmother

comes for me, girl who beat the boy. *A lady never,* hisses Grandmother,

defends herself with fists! What do they teach you in this here school—

fight or Golden Rule? I live by the Rule, but that boy made me cry.

Calling me a slave made my temper blaze; saying it in front of class

made me whip his --ss. Miss Patterson didn't make him finish his work.

Hush your mouth! Stop fighting, especially boys. Just mind your teacher.

Don't cause trouble, grow up to be educated just like your teacher.

I gag and spit. I'd rather die than be that mop-head, I tell Grandmother.

I can't keep coming up here getting you out of trouble. Just do the work.

I don't know what's gotten into you. You used to love school.

Now she'll start, it's your duty, save our race, go to the head of class

sermon on Booker T., W.E.B., Mary Bethune, Dorothy Height, or cry

about sacrifices others made so I can work twice as hard, or cry

about opportunities she never had; never had a white teacher

I think she's blessed. I'll have what she couldn't, hats, gloves, class.
I think to hell with that, but don't let it show. I fear Grandmother
will preach. I wish she could spend one day in my school.
Even if she never fights, never talks, and finishes all her work,

teacher will do her like she does me: sniff her nose, give more work.
No gold star on my 100% papers, but good she can't make me cry.
Crying makes me forget the Rule even though it's not taught in school.
I learn what to wear, swear, style my hair, talk soft so teacher
won't send me to the board in my saddle oxfords wearing a granny-
broomstick dress. Miss Patterson only calls on me during math class.

I am smart, so what is math? Jesus, it is worse in front of the class
sixty eyeballs piercing my back. Long division I cannot seem to work.
My socks slide into my shoes, sash comes undone on my granny-
dress, I try to solve, then with a sob, *I don't know the answer,* I cry.
Stand there until you do, you're so smart barks the teacher.
For fifty minutes kids snicker and point at me, dunce of the school.

Next day Grandmother's wrath storms into math class,
teacher is surprised, says she is wise about her grandchild's work.
I can't hear all, but rag doll hangs her head. I strut home with Grandma.

How Long's the Train Been Gone?

(for J.A.B. 12/08/87)

Grand Baldwin ebony hewn, ivory keyed

Played Harlem spirituals in store-front churches

Majestically bulging in the *Amen Corner*

Sounding too fine—fine-tuned, resonate

Played [W]right in Paris

Brought down moon shattered stars

Stood gracefully in *Giovanni's Room*

Playing *Blues for Mister Charley*

Ah! Music on a grand scale

When you played *Just Above my Head*

Baby grand baldwin squatting low

Intermezzo in a smoky back room

Your mellow-noted rhapsody entered me

Defined my time by your tempo

I felt *The Fire Next Time* I held you

Playing *Sonny's Blues,* you healed old wounds

Maan, *If Beal Street Could Talk*

We'd know the score—

You sounded your native notes allegro

Showed us rainbow-edged dreams

Substances of things hoped for

Evidence of things seen

You told us a story so incredible—

A prophet you, you whom nobody knew

Your name a eeeeeeeeee dooop bop a doop

A beeee bop!

Yours were *Notes of a Native Son*

That echo now, hang heavy in air

Above a vacant stage

Where you were rolled away

No encore for the final curtain call

We couldn't pay *The Price of the Ticket*

So, have you gone now to *Tell it on the Mountain*

In *Another Country*? Or will you hang around

Old stage doors haunting opening nights and still

Somehow playing the blues?

My Brother Jay, A Trilogy

I. In the Eighties, My Brother Jay

Mamma says the worst has happened. It's morning and daddy is
fixing his eggs in the little black skillet. Mamma's eyes are red and
swollen.

She has not combed her hair. She looks like she doesn't care.
Frying eggs spit grease on the chrome stove. Daddy's jaw is set.

His ears go back. *Deserved it*, daddy says. *Damned son-of-a-bitch!*
Mamma drops her juice glass, crashing, blue splinters on the floor.

That's my child you talking 'bout. My son, and I ain't no bitch you
son-of-a-bastard. They don't see me standing near the toaster in my

flannel teddy bear jammies granny sent. I'm shaking and start to cry.
Boy made his bed hard, now he got to lie in it, daddy turns from sink,

pops pepper on his eggs. *Jimmy that's your son you talking 'bout.*
He ain't in the damn bed by himself. We in it too. We all affected.

Mamma's crying, her nose dripping. *The hell you say!* Daddy's temple

veins thump. Mamma sobs, *It's a death sentence. It shouldn't be*

a death sentence. Daddy slams down his fork. *He sinned.* Mamma

shouts, w*e sinned too, but we didn't die. We just got pregnant and*

got married. Is Jay dying? My voice shakes and they both jump and

turn around to me. *James died a long time ago*, daddy mumbles, but

mamma sighs and she pulls me to her coffee breath. *He's sick baby.*

I'm seven, my brother is nineteen and daddy says he can't come

home, and mamma says we're going to get him and bring him home

and daddy can take his ratty ass and go straight to hell. We take the

Greyhound to San Francisco through that gate, it isn't even golden

but red, red as blood Jay spits when he tries to eat, like red snot from

his nose when I give him pepper pot soup. Daddy stays but won't talk

to Jay. Mamma says pay him no mind. Jay's tears slide from his long

lashes. They look like jewels on his face. His cracked lips do not smile.
He can't sing songs off the radio, not even Rapper's Delight. He

sweats. I wipe his face with my Cyndi Lauper cloth until mamma
makes me go to bed. I pray that Jay won't die because he is gay.

Daddy says all gay men die and go to hell. I think heaven is the happy
place. Maybe I'm confused like when I thought the wafer was the

white skin of Jesus and refused to eat it. Maybe happy people go to
hell. The last day of school I come home to see Jay loaded into an

orange and white ambulance, red top rolling, door slams, and it
screeches away down Imperial Highway. Mamma crying, daddy

holding her up. She sees me, grabs my hand *Get my keys. I'm going
with my baby. Come on,* mama says. Daddy won't come. *You old

stubborn fool! May your soul rot in your pious shit.* Mamma backs out
the truck, and we follow the siren's whine to the emergency room

door. Mamma running almost falls but I catch her arm. We wait for
Jay to get a room and daddy comes and we are waiting, and

Jay's friend Jerome comes. Daddy jumps up, socks him in the mouth
knocking out his front teeth and blood and police take daddy away.

Jerome is crying, and mamma is crying, and I am crying. Jay slips
away at eight fifty-two p.m. when it just starts to rain and lightning
streaks windows, thunder rumbles, drowning out mama's screams.

II. In the Eighties, My Son Jay

He looks me dead in my face, my man face and tell me he don't like
girls except to be his good friends, hang out in the mall and all. I'm

not seeing what he means, not knowing what the hell he saying to
me, his daddy. Him smiling, looking like a cat what swallowed the

mouse, licking his lips. He say dad I'm homosexual. I hit the wall with
me fist. Bust hole, a man hole. I taught you to be a man. He steps

back saying, it's just me dad. I am just what I am. Out my house. No nasty shit in here. Okay he says quiet. Hurt catch on the turn of his

thick lips. He looks past me, liquid brown eyes full of regret. My throat dry. My hands sweat. I feel tears freeze in my throat. Why

son? What I do? What I don't do? What I can do? Heavenly Father! He goes down back steps, his mamma starring at me, tell me to stop

him, but I'm the one sending him from here, away from people who know me. I'm done with it two years when my wife come waking me

up with that phone call saying he sick to death. He can't bring that sickness up in here. She curse me. Brings him anyway. What a man

can do? Woman/mamma crazy, wild about her child. She spoil him up. She the one make him weak. She the one. So, I bear the shame.

Disease without a name I tell my friends, and they don't pry. My son, six-foot one, ninety-nine pounds. I pray. I cry. Then I wait for him to die.

III. My Son Jay, In the Eighties

Gorgeous baby, so lovely I always dress him in blue or

people take him for a girl, thick hair curled around his oval

face, almond eyes thick black lashes, cupid lips smiling

whenever he saw me. Walked early, talked before he walked.

Named him James Harrison Walker, for his daddy, but Jimmy

wouldn't let me call him Little Jimmy. We agreed on Jay who grew so

big and tall. He was perfect, so easy to love, talented, artistic, and

perceptive. His father was angry when Jay came out, but I wasn't

caught off guard. I didn't want him to be a macho man. He was love.

A man who would not even kill a fly or stomp an ant. He just wanted

to be free, was so much like me, flesh of my flesh, bone of my bone.

Now he's gone. Just wanted to express himself like anybody else. His

own daddy made him feel like his life and love were wrong, like man

can be only one thing, but my Jay was so fly—my mariposa.

Present Tense

Mrs. Pettawah's Journal Entry,

January 20, 2009

This is the moment of sweet grace and redemption.

From Reconstruction to a new construction of nation-

hood, from out of many, one body under a groove.

This is the time to snatch the blinders off Justice

and let her see how justice is won by just us. See

all that's been done in the name of free democracy.

Hey now, this here is the *second* to heal—so many

didn't live to savor this day—but when I look up

in this cloud-patched sky, I see my husband, Mack,

King and Norma Jean, Malcolm and Rosa, Coretta

and Viola, James and Andrew, Michael and four little girls,

my grandma too and Miss Avery from down the street.

All standing at attention deep in meditation, shining,

beaming their black light, their UV rays down on US.

Orison

June 17, 2015

Our Mother Father God
Do not forgive them this time.

For they know what they do.

They have done it before
Before the Christian Era

Even unto now, in this century
New but filled with pain.

From rugged crosses to poplar trees
From nooses to blazing fires

From Calvary to Charleston
Do not forgive, for we have not

Been delivered from evil.
We have not been saved.

And Yours is the Power
To end crucifixions.

Or have you bequeathed
That power to us?

Amen.

She

She bottles, bottles glass

Translucent as ocean in sunlight

Keeps bottles uniquely shaped

Wine or salsa jars

Green olive oil but no baby

Babies are gone

She bottles Henry, William too

Captures beams washes until

Sparkles are starshine

Some she places in her garden

Upside down a terrarium grows

Holly fern & baby tears

Plant fetcher jars

Bottle light catchers

Candle bottles glass spun

Marrow of her tomorrows

She bottles up loose ends

Empties her tears in jugs

Bottles dreams on a shelf

She bottles, bottles until

Her bottles break.

First

First time, Not.

We suffer first line.

First, we die.

We always dying:

On a cross

In Crusades

On slave ships

On plantations

In trees

Big Houses

Cotton fields

Of fever yellow

Typhoid red

Influenza

Polio

Ebola

SARS

MERS

COVID 19

Of sugar

BP

In childbirth

Our hearts skipping stopping!

Some say it's our fault.

Some say it's theirs.

If a cure comes

We won't get it first.

Some fault racist systems

Some luck of the draw.

This is not a test.

If it were

Answers are

Not true or false

But multiple choice.

We keep coming back.

Who knows how, why

We do we do.

We rarely jump out windows

Slit our own throats

Worship money

Suicide without it

Like deep old rivers

We just keep going on.

Quilt Pieces

A feminine heirloom

When did we begin to know

To really understand

That the women, mommas, grannies, aunties

Were not stone fixtures in our lives

To bolster us up forever?

When did we discover,

Mothers cry saltwater tears?

When did we realize,

Those staunch-backed, broad-shouldered

Soft-lapped women

Who sometimes recalled slavery,

Worked their way through kitchens

Through world wars—

Loved, gave birth during depressions

Ate around fringes of the table

So that we could have enough

Wouldn't be here always?

Those take no mess, I'll

Slap you into next week women:

Tender-hearted, hard-shelled mothers

Those Sunday-go-to-meeting women,

Standing in paten plastic heels

Being ladies on Sunday

Being maids on Monday

Pushing us hard

To "Be somebody" and "Make something

Of ourselves!"

Remembering their own aborted dreams—

Why didn't we know the value of their vision?

Why didn't we heed their woman wisdom?

Those women who could sing a song

Wrapping it around us like swaddling clothes

When did they grow old—their black magic hair

Fade—their clear brown eyes turn misty blue?

We awoke one day

To be who they were.

We are the sturdy-back women now

Our mothers slipped quietly—

When we weren't watching

When we were striving to be different

When we were looking outside ourselves—

Into twilight that blended them among stars.

We can look inside ourselves to find

Quilted patches of their lives and piece

Together a quilt for our winter.

To the African American student who said she didn't connect with Africa apart from the color of her skin

Africa in you is more than your skin's color, honey.

It's the kiss of mountains on your hips

Rising pyramid of your lips

River Niger swaying in your walk

Mango sweetness when you talk your talk.

It's coconut nap in your natural hair

Historical oppression when you sing blues

It's funky drums when you dance your groove.

When you turn yourself into yourself

You'll see the connection

You'll *be* the connection.

All in together, March 2020

We are not all in this together.

Some of *we* are homeless.

Some of *we* lost our jobs.

Some of *we* live on the streets.

Some of *we* are dying.

Some of *we* live in fifty thousand dollar

Underground bunkers

With heated pools, game rooms

Pantries stocked with abundance.

Some of *we* need food, paper towels, toilet paper.

We are not all in this together

Because disease does indeed discriminate

Attacking poor malnourished uninsured

In this world's richest country.

In this country *we* are not all

In this together and I am tired

Of hearing it repeated.

We are the "shit-hole" country now!

Why? On Account of What

10/1/2017

Las Vegas, Twenty-First Century

White people who think

non-whites pose a threat

especially blacks—are

always shocked

when the dangerous

mass murderer

lives next door

in their affluent

neighborhood

probably gated.

They always cry

why why why?

He had everything

white skin, maleness

citizenship, wealth.

Why? Because he could.

For him there was no

stop and frisk

no suspicion of thuggishness

no Zimmerman keeping watch.

He did it because he could

with support of NRA

who thinks gun control

is the same as a vasectomy.

Shadows on the Hills

A cabin in Georgia Mountains

High up on a shelf

An ancient radio just for décor

Nicely adorned place

Black bear moose art

Radio probably purchased at auction

Or flea market roadside

Missing an electrical cord.

Sometime around 2 am

A song burst forth

We thought from TV

But no—music came from

The old brown radio:

Starry starry night

With eyes that know

Know the darkness in my soul

It kept repeating

Playing from 2-4 a.m.

Then suddenly stopped

As it had begun.

Vincent were you visiting

Passing through from *Auvers-sur-Oise*

Slipping from under

A veil of night

Still life doing your impressions

Playing on an old radio?

Wild Sunflowers

Your madness flowers

Coloring canvas

Springing even as you sleep

Burning from your deep

Brightly green or vermeil in sunlight.

On a starry starry night

Shadows inside your gloom

Alone in your lonely room

Gun in hand you could no longer stand

Our blinded eyes that would not see

You took your life away,

Leaving cypress forest, aging couple

Sidewalks with quaint cafes

Sunflowers on a rainy day

You let your Spirit fly away.

Still life will ever stay

As painted fruit upon the tray.

Why I Love Democracy

There is no aristocracy

people are in charge

even when people are wrong.

Stupid people have freedom

to say all sorts of idiotic things

if their idiocy

does not imping on mine.

I can be a fool

get other fools to follow.

In the marketplace of ideas

I can sell bombast for substance, *believe me*

people are free to buy it.

I am free to believe white is right.

Others are free to deny it.

I am free to be leader of the Pac.

Others are free to sack the Pac,

send them back to school

to understand *E pluribus Unum.*

One nation under the sun.

I am free to pray

while others dance the night away.

Unless democracy has room for all

what Nikki said rings true

democracy becomes demon-ocracy

where devils reign and each citizen

looks, thinks, and acts the same.

The Forget

Battled bombed bedraggled

Sun sets on uncollected trash

Broken bottle cuts a child

A revolution is coming

Forget will go on forgetting

Each time marigolds bloom or

Teenagers fall in love

The forget keeps forgetting

Our valley of dry bones

Beneath an ocean of florescent

Sharks soaking in our melanin

Roses still are red

Like black man-child blood

On concrete streets

In broad daylight

A revolution is coming

Was said to have come

Is still to come

When bacon stops frying

When we love tofu

When the forget

Stops forgetting

Sorrow leaves a canebrake

Forget-me-not blooms against a sea wall

When people the day

Before yesterday

Become people the day

After tomorrow

Our great forget will not

Be forgotten.

After Orlando

How queer our voices are

When we explain hate

How queer the other side of love is

In a pristine green blue globe of life

How utterly ugly lackluster convoluted

A heart how it cracks attacks cracks

How queer a world queering how

Queer the children's questions

Our queer answers

We are all queer—we died there

A Disneyworld away in toilet stalls

Dancing on a floor queerly dodging

Killjoy

We know it matters not who we love

Just that we love   not who we kiss

Or how   just that lips meet in human longing.

God is queer queerest Spirit in us

Only we can transmute hate to love

From straight and narrow

To a wide-open queer world

Of peace joy power

Geraniums

After 9/11 I come to see your mom.

Years ago, we brought a huge snapping turtle
to her pond where it lived for decades.

Now her pond is dry, overgrown with dandelions.
Wild geraniums clinging to cracked clay pots

bleed their red into ninety degrees of smog-filled
sun shining off the Spanish tile rooftop.

Her shades are drawn, doorbell's broken, hanging
out of its socket. I knock twice.

A morning glory vine twists through the entry arch,
wooden door cracks, her face opens.

Hugs, how've you been—it's in her eyes
the slight smie sliding over her false teeth.

I haven't seen her since San Jose—
reunion you didn't attend.

She finds a photo album there in the room
where we ate our stolen Hostess cupcakes

there on that sofa, we sit thumbing through.
Suddenly you look up at me eyes dancing.

It's our eighth-grade picture:
Billy Ross cuts in line between us.

You laugh and we forget our practiced smiles.

Your mother makes tuna sandwiches.
I remember it's Friday. She chops onions,

and boiled eggs, spreads mayo on white bread.
I don't tell her I'm vegan. She places before me

a school lunch: potato chips, pickle
and orange juice.

I eat like a twelve-year old.
We talk of many things

with you perched on her shoulder.
She carries you on her back.

When I leave, she hugs me tight
longingly. Down three steps

past the pond, Geraniums
bleed into sun.

Stripes and Stars

They give her mother an American flag
bunched tight into a triangle
like the body they deliver full of holes
knotted cold never to mambo.

Her girl thought goodness would shield
never believed evil was real— fought for
some foreign freedom— in a place
that forced veiled faces, covered heads.

Yes, there she went.

Struggle here, her mother begged.

But no, she would go, volunteer.

Now she's home with flattened flag.
Her mother shakes and scrapes black
stripes from a stuffed zebra white
vinegar won't wash clean.

They say good things about her girl
her mother knows are lies. She meets
her daughter's stare in the scrubbing
of the childhood toy.

Brown eyes full of wonder
brown skin gone ash.
Zebra! The mother cries.

Confederate Flap

There it is, red

Like some necks,

White, like some hands,

Blue, like some eyes,

With bars like jails

And stars that shine

From a billy club

Upside the head.

There it is,

A dividing cloth

On Freedom's table.

Somebody please,

Say grace.

Prayer

She knew prayer

was the heart-felt longing of the soul,

but what her soul longed for

was somehow unholy, ungodlike

somehow not like the god

she'd learned to serve in childhood's hour:

great white father, gleaming so pure.

This longing in her soul was black,

like evil preached about on Sunday mornings

or grime left on unclean clothes.

This thing—

this prayer within her

wanted nothing more than to feel

the presence of the Negro

wanted to feel the "everted lips, short

thick nappy hair."

She prayed out loud to be

"Honest, decent, pure, innocent—"

but prayer, she knew

was the heart-felt longing of her soul.

From George

(1973-2020)

I am surprised. I'd rather be alive

See my children grow but it's nice to know

The world won't let my murder go, no jive

I appreciate what your protests show.

These killer cops you'll have to overthrow.

When he held me in his grip, he knew me.

I realized I'd seen him too, I know.

Tried with all my might to get him to see

He's killing me, crushing me with his knee.

Wonder when we'll be seen as citizens?

We fought in every war to make them free.

Our black necks they pop and ring like chickens.

My voice ghost with others killed by police.

Racial oppression and hatred must cease.

Future Tense

The One

I'm a seventh daughter of a seventh mother
Born on this continent. First in 1777, delivered herself
slid out when her mama jumped overboard.
Saved by a sailor man who named her Sea, set her
to work in the islands soon as she could walk.

I'm the seventh one of seven sisters who saw seven
years of bad luck in a cracked up looking glass
on a seven-foot wall smeared with woman blood.

Sarah had babies, every one, but one, still born.
In 1807 Esther lives, a seven-month wonder
slept on her mama's side as Sarah cut cane.

Esther in 1827 bore the one with gray eyes, the one
who sat beside the sea counting sunshine seeds.
In 1857 this gray-eyed gal, name Sophia, gets
Septima, her long legs kick midwife Annie.

She's the one had freedom's baby in 1887. Named
that girl Liberty. Liberty went to Spelman, married
a professor old enough to be her daddy. He lived
to see Senna born in 1907, but Liberty left for Leslie
a brown-eyed, leggy woman who lived for a thrill.

My mama came in 1937, Senna named her Surely
which mama changed to Shirley soon as she could.
In the Sixties, I'm the one she names Spirit Rose.

I'm the one walked the seven hills in Cincinnati
I'm seven times seven to the power of seventy.

Future *is* the palm of my hand.

Acknowledgements

"Prayer" (poem). *Excavating Honesty: An Anthology of Rage and Hope in America.* Lisa Mangini and Talisha Shelley, Eds. 2017.

"Strut." *Obsession: Sestinas in the Twenty-First Century.* Eds. Carolyn Beard Whitlow and Marilyn Krysl. Lebanon, NH: Dartmouth UP, 2014.

"My Brother Jay: A Trilogy," *A Face to Meet Faces: An Anthology of Contemporary Persona Poetry,* Ed. Stacey Lynn Brown and Oliver De la Paz. Akron, Ohio: U of Akron Press, 2012.

"Mrs. Pettawah's Journal Entry, January 20, 2009." *44 on 44: Forty-Four African American Writers on the Election of Barak Obama 44th President of the United States.* Eds. Lita Hooper, Sonia Sanchez, Michael Simanga. Chicago: Third World Press, 2011.

"Geraniums," "Stars and Stripes," *Drumvoices Revue,* v.16, no. 1&2, Spring-summer-fall 2008.

"Frederick Douglass to Three Young Men, Waiting," in *The Ringing Ear: Black Poets Lean South,* Nikky Finney, Ed. Athens: University of GA Press, 2007.

"Silver Rights," in *Gathering Ground,* Eds. Toi Derricotte and Cornelius Eady, Ann Arbor: University of Michigan Press, 2007.

First Edition: 2020
Rs. 200/-

Cyberwit.net
HIG 45 Kaushambi Kunj, Kalindipuram
Allahabad - 211011 (U.P.) India
http://www.cyberwit.net
Tel: +(91) 9415091004 +(91) (532) 2552257
E-mail: info@cyberwit.net

Printed at Repro India Limited.